Seasons of the Year

Delphine Kalinowski

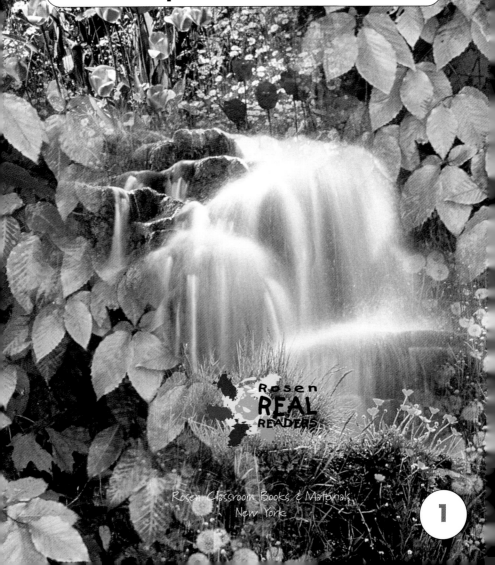

Rosen
REAL
READERS

Rosen Classroom Books & Materials
New York

1

There are four seasons in the
year.

In the spring, we see new leaves.

In the summer, we go to the beach.

In the fall, we rake leaves.

In the winter, we make a snowman.

Then it is spring again!

Words to Know

beach

leaves

rake

snowman